nearly FLORIDA

nearly FLORIDA

James Brock

ANHINGA PRESS, 2000
TALLAHASSEE, FLORIDA

Copyright © James Brock 2000

All rights reserved under
International and Pan-American Copyright Conventions.

No portion of this book may be reproduced in any form without
the written permission of the publisher, except by a reviewer,
who may quote brief passages in connection with a review
for a magazine or newspaper.

Cover illustration by Beverly Rhoads

Author photograph – U. L. Keys
Book design and production – Lynne Knight

Library of Congress Cataloging-in-Publication Data
nearly Florida by James Brock – First Edition
ISBN 0938078-67-4
Library of Congress Cataloging Card Number – 00-105327

*This publication is sponsored in part by a grant from the Florida Department of State,
Division of Cultural Affairs, and the Florida Arts Council.*

Anhinga Press Inc. is a nonprofit corporation dedicated wholly
to the publication and appreciation of fine poetry.

For personal orders, catalogs and information write to:
Anhinga Press
P.O. Box 10595
Tallahassee, FL 32302
Web site: www.anhinga.org
E-mail: info@anhinga.org

Published in the United States by Anhinga Press, Tallahassee, Florida.
First Edition, 2000

*for Gerri,
    my familiar*

 Contents

Acknowledgments   ix

I. Boise/Indiana

Voices on the Air   3
The Recognition of Beasts   5
The Growth of Mathematics   6
A Wedding Proposal   8
Tornado Warning   10
Creation Ex Nihilo: On Our First Anniversary   13
Craters of the Moon. 82 mph   15
Still Life   16
A Young Poet's Portrait   18
The First Roentgenogram   20
The Aviary: Midnight   21

II. north, California

Love and Its Locked Houses   25
To the coroner who did not have to draw my blood   26
When Loss Attends Passion   28
After we have talked   29
95 Ft. Down   30
Marcella's Homestead, Dickson, Tennessee   32
Marcella's Homestead II   34
A Stand of Aspen   35
Rehearsal: Christmas Eve   36
Lucifer Unemployed   37
Tom   40
The Pink Palace   42
I Wish I Could Skate Across the Wide, Frozen River   43
The Drunken Comet   45
The Pope Arrives in Denver   47

III. Beyond the Coast of Nashville, the Desert of Idaho

The Bad Cartographer   51
On the Maps of Creativity   52
Traces   53
The Good Uncle   55
In the Hospital of Broken Rules:
    Optic Ward, Children's Wing   56
Girl at the Hotel Exile   58
Gloucester and Edgar at Dover   59
The Second Sky   60

IV. Florida, Where We Are Heading

Lover's Key, Florida   63
The Cartography of Oranges   65
The Residual Boy   67
My Grand Cayman Dog   69
In fifth position,   71
A Little Gershwin   72
Her Disrobing   73
Burial   74
Hurricane. North Dakota   75
She Sleeps Under Florida   77
What Is Uncharted Remains   79
Florida, at the End of Time   81
The Bougainvillea, Your Black Dress   83
Island Park: Midnight   85

About the author   89

Acknowledgments

I wish to express my gratitude to the editors of the following magazines and the anthology in which these poems (some in early formations) first appeared:

Alaska Quarterly Review: "Creation Ex Nihilo: On Our First Anniversary," "Love and Its Locked Houses," and "Tornado Warning"

Caffeine Destiny: "Hurricane. North Dakota"

Chili Verde Review: "The Second Sky"

Cincinnati Poetry Review: "Craters of the Moon. 82 mph"

cold-drill: "95 Ft. Down"

College English: "The Growth of Mathematics"

Colorado-North Review: "Gloucester and Edgar at Dover"

Fresh Ground: "The Drunken Comet"

Idaho's Poetry: A Centennial Anthology, edited by Ron McFarland and William Studebaker, The University of Idaho Press. Copyright © 1989: "The Growth of Mathematics," "The Recognition of Beasts"

Jacaranda Review: "Girl at the Hotel Exile"

Kansas Quarterly: "The Pink Palace"

Kimera: "The Residual Boy," "Traces"

Louisville Review: "The Recognition of Beasts"

Mangrove: "The Bougainvillea, Your Black Dress," "Tom"

Northwest Review: "To the coroner who did not have to draw my blood"

The Panhandler: "Still Life"

Permafrost: "After we have talked," "I Wish I Could Skate Across the Wide, Frozen River"

Red Booth Review: "Florida, At the End of Time," "The Pope Arrives in Denver," "When Loss Attends Passion"

Red Rock Review: "Her Disrobing," "In fifth position"

Santa Barbara Review: "The Bad Cartographer"

Seattle Review: "The First Roentgenogram"

Scarlet Letters: "What Is Uncharted Remains"

Southern Ocean Review (NZ): "A Little Gershwin," "Rehearsal: Christmas Eve"

Sucarnochee Review: "The Aviary: Midnight," "Lucifer Unemployed," "A Stand of Aspen," "A Wedding Proposal"

Sun Dog: The Southeast Review: "A Young Poet's Portrait"

Sycamore Review: "Voices on the Air"

Talking River Review: "The Good Uncle"

Three Candles: "Island Park: Midnight"

Timberline: "Marcella's Homestead, Dickson, Tennessee," "Marcella's Homestead II"

I also wish to recognize the National Endowment for the Arts, the Alex Haley Foundation, the Tennessee Arts Commission, and the Idaho Commission for the Arts for fellowships which supported the writing of many of these poems.

And in my travels through the visible geographies, I thank my landlocked teachers and poet-friends, with whom I started, Roger Mitchell, Philip Appleman, Don Boes, Dan Bourne, Tyler Fleeson, Robyn Wiegman, Monica Barron, Keith Ratzlaff, Dean Young, and Kevin Stein. Thank you, too, Beverly Rhoads, sweet and talented friend. My appreciation to Julia Levine, Larry Johns, and Joann Gardner for their careful and intelligent reading of my manuscript. And to my current fellow-travelers, Bruce Gatenby, Jesse Millner, Lyn Millner, Steve Donachie, and Nora Donachie, your company makes all the difference.

nearly FLORIDA

I will rest my love on whom I love.

— *Muriel Rukeyser*

I. Boise/Indiana

> Next time, for sure,
> I'll stay and let the real thing take
> the place of reminiscence.
>
> — *Diane Raptosh*

Voices on the Air

From a radio station in Missouri,
an escaped murderer was on the call-in line,
her voice distant, a box within
a box. The talk-show host, imagining the publicity
if he could trace the call, stalled. "Lady,
I got to break for station identification.
It's an F.C.C. thing." She came back
and recalled Lawton, Oklahoma,
how she killed her husband and two boys, how
a good hunting knife enters the body
clean, as if the body were a pillow.
"But it takes a fat man," she said, "like
my husband with his fat, hairy belly."
The host pumped her. Why, why? He wanted
a Satan worshipper, an abused wife, or better
a man-hater who revenged her sex upon a husband
and two sons ready to betray her. "No,"
she insisted. "It was the loneliness,
the inequities of despair."
In the studio, the host nodded
to his technician. "We got her? Good," he said
on the air. She stayed on the phone, talking,
humming. Humming, I turned off the radio
in my car and looked into the dark
Idaho desert, my eyes reflecting white
on the glass, the lights on a radio tower
signaling red. No outside talk
could come in, except for the ghost
that I would slip into someday,
a rattle in my heart. The world drove on,
inconsolable with hate, murder, and grief:
a man and woman, strangers talking
into a static nothing. Sometimes
the noise at night wakes me. The night before,
it was my neighbor, an eighty-year-old insomniac,

watering her daffodils and morning glories
at three a.m. I turned in bed, alone, the woman
I loved somewhere out a further west, maybe driving
at that moment, hearing the same inexorable
longing I was hearing, the sound of travelers
working their way out of the past. "When we die,"
the murderer said, "we become angels." I turned,
again, and listened to an aged body
bending to a spigot, releasing a spray of water
on the dark earth, and raising her winged voice
in the night air, singing to the flowers,
electric and needful.

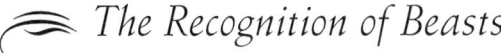 ## The Recognition of Beasts

Beneath Lake Stanley, the kokanee run, red
extinction deep in olive water. Lodgepole
and ponderosa soldier the lake; what can hold
this together? Not the redfish, spent dead
in instinct, not the Sawtooths, this shiver
of granite, nor forests, nor swallows,
nor us. What ordering we impose hollows
experience. To discover a river
from which we came and name it is the wrong
way to force love. Nothing's saved from what we
devise. Then remember the deer struck blind
by our lantern — the white-tailed doe and fawn
frozen, one body paralyzed — as we
recognize our paralysis, our one mind.

# The Growth of Mathematics

Every electric kernel of light
that shimmers from a falling wave
is held by an equation that assumes
all variables: gravity, wind,
inertia. If we stop everything,
the curve may be as pure and certain
as $y + \sin x$. But this is the white love
of self-evident axioms: somewhere
nearing the speed of light, all lines
converge out of necessity.

Today, my love, I have read twelve
love poems by my students,
so many little cartoons of a big heart
to contend with, so many refrigerators
two-thirds empty, windows
over oceans. Waves upon
waves. So what wave shall I proffer
you? Here I could point to our cats,
as tame as love, watching a nuthatch
upside-down. I could offer
you an egg, warm and almost liquid with life,
in your hand. I could give you something.

Walking to the university, I hold
your books, your arm resting like need
around my waist. Somewhere off Alaska,
my friend Tyler tries to forget
his aunt, the nuclear physicist, by chasing
salmon, the trawl lines slack. Somewhere
in Nebraska, two men younger than I
wait near a missile silo, their shift
beginning. If I could, I'd find

a truer arithmetic, or something
that would define the curve
of your arm, there, the presence,
the wave of your body.

A Wedding Proposal

        What shall occur may
pass as the shifting continent
  of sleep, or the lapse
        in weather, or the most
interminable nothing

        save for what memory is
or isn't. What country or cloud
  our marriage I cannot
        predict. It's not
that I lost

        nerve, but trust in sight.
In my memory, I once counted
  the bodies of snow flakes
        and gulls on Montauk:
white ebbing

        white. The sky opened
gray, godless over the Atlantic. Yet
  I know I never saw
        an ocean that impoverished,
that hopelessly

        still. All that can be
measured must have already happened,
  must be logged in the past.
        In a grace which refuses
to be remembered,

>   you and I live
> without measure, born thirteen years
>   after the atomic bomb
>   haloed over Japan.
> We've been past
>
>   our time all our lives.
> We own no day to seize and ravish,
>   and our past will be obliterated
>   as quickly as the future
> flashes out.
>
>   Let us then wed
> after a long engagement, not to mold
>   memory into a thing, but to touch
>   our way through.

Tornado Warning

In confluences
of storm, the wind, as though
  it had bones,
battered the earth. My wife
somewhere else in a library

    bomb shelter
would be safe, at least
  that is what
our neighbor tenants said,
persuading me to leave the

    apartment. I
considered that I would abandon
  to a barometric
nothing our rented home of unquiet
seasons. And what did I salvage?

    I picked up
the day's mail (a bill, a postcard)
  and escaped
to wait out the storm
in the cellar. While my friends

    opened the windows
above me, I left myself
  to the inchoate
currents of desire. What, what
for? I thought. Wind begins

    with the sunder
of heat and cold, the pull
  of opposites:
land and water, mountain and
valley, night and day. Wherever

      wind lifts,
it carries the names it touches.
   For example,
the cool Pacific Trades funnel
into the San Juan winds over

     Puget Sound,
and the wind circles north,
   shouldering east;
Chinook falling from the Palouse,
drifting south, and it collapses

    on itself,
gathering and rising, a tide
   that fills Nevada:
the Santa Ana. Every April,
the month of midwest tornados

     these western winds
climb. Underground in the variances
   of shadow and
longing — how the night before
during the thunderstorm, my wife's

     breasts were tender
dream to my touch, how the heat
   lightning that pulsed
in the darkness and the thick
rain that pelted the windows

     suggested no grief,
only a subtler electricity — memory
   kept me wanting
and wanting. My neighbors returned
with fruit and supplies. We bent

         our darkening heads
to the voice in the radio,
   cupping our ears
against the sirens, "The storm
is bearing northeast on a line

         from Bedford
to Columbus." We were west. What
   then could I fear
except the climb into a brooding
world, its clutch of calm air?

Creation Ex Nihilo:
On Our First Anniversary

> In the beginning, there was nothing, and in that void subatomic particles would appear and disappear. Once in this vacuum genesis, subatomic particles appeared and stayed, and weak and strong forces manifested, expanding those particles, generating more, and finally collapsing ... forming the matter for the Big Bang. I know it doesn't sound plausible, but it only had to happen once.
> — *Jacob Bronowski*

I walk into the autumn; the leaves
of Pin Oak, Dogwood, and Walnut
fragrant with decay and mold comfort
me. Among the biology of death, among
the fallen bracken, the dry purple braize,
and the wintering animals, a man
can think of love, a last resistance
to perfect numbers. It is October, and I
have been married to Annette for one year.

Beginnings are indistinguishable in a universe
out of nothing. From nothing, everything starts.
Yet I know science does not measure
nature, but fabricates only models. Platonic
and post-Einsteinean maps of existences
and events. We are not beings. We live
as events. Everything happens.

Still the universe collapses on itself; bubbles
of it have nudged one another
into oblivion. We too will come
to nothing, despite our atomic structures

as old as the sun. The universe
is the only thing dying more slowly than we are.

A man can think of love
and mark beginnings. I think of Christmases:
When I was fourteen in Boise, my father,
two brothers, and I snowshoed
through the Payette National Forest — waxwings
laced the sky crazy above our noise —
where we felled one blue spruce.
That memory is complete, petrified and uncolored,
ready to disappear in my father's, my brothers'
and my common dying. How can we believe
in beginnings? What begot the present
was unlikely to occur, yet one start
is as good as any other.

This year, Annette and I bought
our first Christmas tree from an ice slick
lot at a Bloomington shopping mall:
a four-foot Douglas Fir, a bad tree
for ornaments, but we bought it
because I thought I smelled something
familiar in its dying. Once the tree's good
side was trimmed with red decorations and
a paper star, I knew all creation
had led up to that event as it leads
up to every event, and I have learned
to mark the daily beginnings in my own life:
the utility bills I pay on the first
of the month, the names of the children
my wife and I have picked. It isn't
a matter of correct living, for I must knead
the substance of my own understanding
each day, for nothing ever ends, for in a universe
bent on disappearing, all events are privileged.

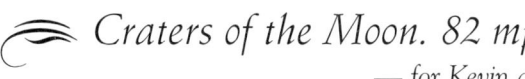 *Craters of the Moon. 82 mph*
— for Kevin and Bruce

One theory holds that life is a mirage of ruin,
where the ship we wave to, to save our drowning,
is a reflection of light and heat and vapor,
where the branch we cling to, to keep our sinking
necks above the quicksand, is only an unrooted stick,
ungrounded to anything solid. For instance, take us,
the three men here, at the Craters of the Moon
National Monument, beyond the nuclear waste sites,
beyond the potato fields leafing green on the lava
basin, beyond the archeological digs of paleolithic
horses, elephants, and cats. The snow flurries
about us this April. The snow falls on our shoulders,
into our faces, and we laugh because we do not
know how we arrived, except at a speed of 82 mph,
too slow to escape any ruinous memory, too slow
to outrun the teenaged girls of our youth who caught
hell from their fathers for us, caught in the tangle
of legs and language that spoke of escape routes
out of deserts worse than any Idaho. Where are we,
these three men, driving to? Who is to say how far
into a world we would go where there is such dying,
such laughing, into a world of so much cinder and
smoke? Who is to say we will not return because
we cannot drive any better but to wreck headlong
into a brick wall that will evaporate at the very last
second? It is not the mirage that worries us. What
are we? Okay, I will tell you. We are three men caught
in wind and time, caught in the piss and creak
of middle age, caught in everything just before
our eyes. We have the nerve to reach toward any branch
and death-grip the limb, knowing nothing is there.
Or rather, we place a hand on the warm, broad
back of our fellow, and what disappears is all
the driving that got us here in the first place.

Still Life

A catalogue would suffice:
a cut-lead crystal bowl,
silver and glass salt and pepper
shakers, two brass candlesticks,
all upon a mahogany drop-leaf
table. From that point, it becomes
a matter of accuracy or art,
whether these wedding gifts
be accounted as properties
for inheritance or as objects
that shape the world. No
matter. The artist has
no children, and he is tired
of the way light is indispensable
to form.   It is evening, and when
he looks out the window, he sees
nothing: the one light washes out
all outside, yellowing the glass
and the walls, locking him within
the walls, leaving him to name
the furniture. Here, he extends
the catalogue: man in chair
at table, sleeping black cat
on the floor.   Someplace else
in the world, his wife also sleeps.
Her room is dark. In the world
he loves, the real world, is
nothing but living. Last night after
they had made love, he understood
how love invents our bodies. We
are birds, he thinks, Matissean

herons that lean
into the waves of air, that leave
the earth in sweeps of green
and blue.
                He locks his mind
on the still life, the catalogue
he must study and shape. The artist
is alone. The sleeping cat
by the radiator remains a cat.

A Young Poet's Portrait

At this moment,
a woman who speaks
French draws your portrait
with a pen. In it, your
head is tilted down, almost
in prayer or sleep.
She leaves your eyes
open. You have never looked
so stern, your stare
so hard. When
you see the portrait, you
think she has captured
something of you, what
your friends ought to know.
Your fingers in the drawing
are long like in an El Greco;
they are bent, grasping
an envelope postmarked
8 Avril Roulle de Croix.
Although you do not
read French, you know
the letter contains
a pidgin gesture of
charity, the way she left
your body a shadow
of a boy you knew at sixteen.
You can hear the tatter
of broken French: *les hommes,
ils ne sont rien.* Words
pretty enough for poetry.
Then let me tell you
this: no woman is drawing
you. Still, you long

for those long, painted
fingers or the invention
of a letter, that somehow poems
were gifts to you from a French
woman. On your own, you resort
to fists in your poems.
You are ashamed what weak
aberrations they make. Once,
while unfolding your hands
you learned to love the familiar.

The First Roentgenogram

He ordered her to lay her hand flat upon the photographic
    plate, but in the dark
of her husband's laboratory — fetid of acids
    and electricity — she
could not unbend her own fear or the arthritis
    in her knuckles. Even
his assistants, four students quick and keen with answers,
    admitted they did not know
its nature, this light of a different intensity.
    X Stahlen, they called it.
Still, how could she not say yes to Wilhelm who,
    at fifty, had realized himself.
Darling, he said to her, *I shall make immortal your hand.*
    Your hand will be sequined
with light. Your hand will be more alive than any hand
    painted by Monet. I am your artist.
He said this, grasping her wrist, forcing her hand down
    slow upon the steely glass.
In the photograph, her living bones blackened, her flesh
    burned invisible on paper,
only her wedding ring — a star that whitened itself out —
    refracted the x-ray. Wilhelm
framed and hung the roentgenogram in his study; he entitled
    it: His Wife's Hand, 1895.

She told her sister that other women would soon come to admire
    Wilhelm's chef d'oeurve,
asking him to take their portraits, and he smiling, would consent,
    wealthy with subjects,
a gallery of high cheek bones, femurs, and crooked
    spines. Only once in her life
did she dare to place her hand over the hand in the x-ray. She
    could not believe her hand
had been so small, that here was a love any light could touch,
    and she lifted her hand,
as if from cupping a husband's face, into the visible air.

The Aviary: Midnight

A desire wakens me. Sounds —
something like rain dying out — rise
from the aviary beneath our bedroom.
I hear the birds' dulling chatter:
the Brazilian cardinals and purple finches,
aroused, sing to calm themselves. Impotent,
I have known the immunities of darkness,
its coolness like the rain that relieves
a fevered world. My wife remains sleeping.
The birds are calling me back
to their own listless flight of sleep.
My back touches her back; my ankle
rests upon her calf. If I turn to her,
it is because a second world calls me.

II. north, California

> It is hard to *find* California now, unsettling to wonder how much of it was merely imagined or improvised; melancholy to realize how much of anyone's memory is no true memory at all but only the traces of someone else's memory.
>
> — *Joan Didion*

Love and Its Locked Houses

To my neighbor, I suggest divorce from a man
who constricts love and grief to a period,
and she thinks it over the coffee
I poured for her, cupping her hand over the surface,
the steam escaping between her fingers, coiling
around her face. She says she is alive
to suffer: a teenager who hates
and a husband who sleepwalks dim
the white-sided air in her house. *I have
too many locks*, she says, *I have too many
shut doors.*
              And it's true: she has earned
bitterness, whether sought for or delivered
unto her. In her former life — twenty years ago —
she had been raped by one of Somoza's elite,
for being a church worker who had taken a wrong turn
on a prison tour, for seeing the grid
of cages, the men stacked in cells
smaller than coffins. Even while her rapist's unshaven
face razed her cheek, even while he cursed her,
Bitch, you fuck no good, she still witnessed:
the hissing of diseased breathing, the air sweating
with dysentery, the smell of men's flesh
turning to iron.
              Will you divorce? I ask.
I don't know, she shakes her head,
the littler infidelities of a husband are criminal
enough. Yet in the cages of her marriage
and house, she has fleshed out love yes by yes.
She asks of me the same question: will you ever start
loving yourself and leave your husband? I confess
that my own grief-gripped heart remains undilated,
that sometimes after I have made love,
I cry because loss attends all passion. She puts
the cup to her lips to quiet me, to release
me from whatever is too easy to say.
She whispers to us: *come out, you can come out now.*

To the coroner who did not have to draw my blood

sixteen years ago, and centrifuge
the alkaline hydrocarbons from my blood,
contributing to the Ada County records
another fact concerning how much gasoline
is too much for the teenaged male
to ingest, who did not have to split
me open, to remove what remained
of the liver, or to cut the lung tissue
to recover the amount of fluid that bled
through the membrane, who did not have
to decide between suffocation or poisoning,
all the while I was pounding the door
of God's speakeasy, having arrived without
the password for the two eyes that hid
behind the door slit and that rolled *oh
brother* when I guessed "Rimbaud's three-legged
cat," and the eyes' voice said, "Get lost,
kid," so I left thinking what a piss-ant
job for an angel, coming back to the world,
my parents' garage, puking something blue
and thin onto the pavement, I give my thanks
to you, as I know you would have been
tender for this late adolescent, whose torso
had just lengthened to man-size, whose
hands were strengthening, whose skin
stretched young and fluid, for you
would have whispered, "Goddamn it,"
with the incision, remembering your own
son, or yourself, and I give you
thanks, for I may be the one you
blessed when you once cursed over

that old man's drink, a Manhattan, "If there
would be one suicide who didn't come
my way," and I tell you now it was me
who didn't come your way, cold, blue,
youthful, rotted, who today rose
with his beloved from the Modoc Lava Caves,
whose bearings were lost in the desert
afternoon light haloing silver off
automobiles and asphalt and ash.

When Loss Attends Passion

After I pulled out of you, our
bodies pearled with semen
and sleep, you whispered,
*I know their name. They're
tangerines, not oranges.* And I
knew your meaning, what you
have added. I used to believe
that every accumulation and each
accretion of love meant a losing.
But your room — this peach light,
this filling incense, these sheets,
this window emptying its diffuse
gray upon your face — and I cannot
bear to think of love
as any kind of losing, except
for the usual stuff that decays
into softening, the aftermath
and afterfigures of our sex, the
expired vulnerabilities that we hide
with compliments of good sex. And
you tell me they're tangerines, and you
kiss me, here, in this quieting of air
we shelter, where we are healed,
wholed, held.

After we have talked

about me, and after you have spoken
of your past lovers, whom you neither
named nor called lover, and after you
have told me that you never
said to a man, *I love you*,
I did not believe you at first,
until later, after I first
disentangled your clothes from you,
letting them slide to the floor
from your bed, after I kissed
your throat, first mistaking
your pain and release as lust,
until I heard you say,
"I can't believe this," meaning
exactly that, and I understood
then, *never pry, but only
pain and release*, and I never
wanted to know any man's
name whom you did not love.
I do not remember the first
time you said you loved me.
Rather I think of our empty clothes,
the entwined aftermaths of a man
turning toward a woman he loves
a woman toward a man she loves,
and the air so saturated with light
and spring, our clothes touched us,
ginger, to our skin as we dressed each
other, eager to do this again, soon.

95 Ft. Down

These days I awake
to the used grievances
of love, that I have
not gotten very far,
or very free. And I confess,
my lover, that I am 33,
and this night alone
I feel my belly press
against the rusted beams
of the Jefferson Street
Bridge which this city is
going to blow up anyway.
My best guess is
ninety-five feet down,
a number you gave me
in your story about how
you went diving, miles out
in the gray gulf, a depth
where you could die
a dozen ways: on top,
it is the swells that slap
you against the rudder, or
fifteen feet below,
the currents that tear
you from the anchor line,
or just the descent, where
the darkness alone is enough
to kill, or it is the ascent
that can go bad, especially
if your buddy insists on
the pink air tank, the cute
one, and she runs out
of air because the tank
is too small, the narks

shaking her and you
into delirium as you share
your air and as you try
not to come up too fast,
too urgently, lest you
rip your lungs. And while
you're down that deep, what
do you see? Only eels
phosphorescent, thin, hungry
in the distance, the only
light beyond your torch.

Marcella's Homestead, Dickson, Tennessee

Marcella is the only woman
I have known who has kissed
Elvis, and I imagine it had
to occur after "I Want to Play
House with You," after
the King sang the lines,
"I'd rather see you dead, little girl,
than be with another man,"
and I asked you, Marcella's daughter,
where was she kissed —
Tahoe? Vegas? Honolulu? No,
on the lips, stupid ... and
that's the joke I recall,
as Marcella frames us with
her camera, before her old homestead,
the tar-paper intact,
the wallpaper still radiant violet,
abandoned in 1959, Elvis overseas
then, and Marcella heading west.
I am ready for Marcella to say
"Smile." And I do, thinking
of that joke. Or maybe it is you
I think of, how the disaffection
of air and light leaves our bodies
estranged and new, how I long to kiss
you, how I would rather see you
alive, possible, even with another
man, how self-pity washes
from me when I hold your hips,
your shuddering falling away, and
when the words I whisper
to you are no longer divisible,

distressed. But all that Marcella
does is wave her hand above
the camera, brushing the air, saying,
"There, there, hold it,"
as the shadows of sugar maple
and oak abrade our faces with
a lightness we readily bear.

Marcella's Homestead II

Following the property line, we came
upon a holler, a smooth vulva
of earth that gave over to a plot
of tobacco, a house, a small pasture.
Your mother and aunt walked quickly
down, clipping themselves to their pasts,
and there at the house they spoke to
a woman and her father, who had
heard of the Jones place, that up there
was a truckful of pretty girls. You
and I held back a little, standing
apart, until the woman's daughters, maybe
ages six and eleven, drew us in.
The older one with only a sun dress
and sandy hair came to you, said,
"You're beautiful." You thanked
her, and then we asked to see
her horse and dog, and the girls
told us about their daddy, how he'd be
home soon from the tool and die
shop. Before we left, their mother
looked at your hair, and then
pointed to her younger daughter,
her hair red and full and human,
and said, "Hair like that will get her
into boy trouble." Returning to
the homestead, I wanted to amend what
the mother had said, or what her daughter
might have meant, or what I had hidden
within my own silence, admitting I am
hewn by your beauty amid these falling
poplars and oaks. But here were
children only, waiting for their father
to come home, a wife also waiting
for her husband, everyone waiting
for a slow turn of love to arrive
autumnal and settle on this land.

A Stand of Aspen

When nightfall extinguishes the last
light, when lovers can no longer
see the stand of aspen in December
that so confirms their love with
its nakedness that betrays no infirmity,
I begin to believe that I have had
too much love slashing and burning
and running. I want to light afire
the night and the aspen and the stars
with sparks as hot as the sun, and
see it all whiten with heat as the stand
collapses, smoldering on the frozen
ground. But this time I will stay
with you, to wait out the clearing
smoke, to claim that it was no
accident that had happened here, and
to watch for the seedlings to appear
from the bracken. With you, I will
bring them water. With you, I will
bring them some light.

Rehearsal: Christmas Eve

Ten degrees and dark afternoon,
and you go outside into the Jeep
to rehearse your song for the reunion.
All I can see is you huddled over
the car stereo, adjusting the volume,
pushing back the seat. All I guess
is that it must be *The Christmas
Song*, something older than we are,
in a brassy timbre. I lean
to the kitchen window and tap
silently against the shouldering
clear of this night. When you
hit the lower registers, I swear
I feel the window vibrate,
the wind throwing its ice
upon the glass. When you come
in, I know better than to ask
how it went, but still when I kiss
you, I touch your face, run
my fingers soft over the pulsing
warmth of your throat, and you
catch me wanting, in that old,
male way, wanting to know, and
you say, *It's a gift, you know.
That's all. Something you wait for.*

Lucifer Unemployed

I.

It's enough that the other
archangels are out of work —
how cheesy they are — Beelzebub
lying on the unemployment
insurance claim form, how
he was fired without due cause;
Mammon eyeing the destitute
teenager, thinking that it
wasn't his idea to line up
on election day, 1992, hearing
the girl say she would vote
for Perot, if at all, if she
were old enough. Lucifer
has hit it hard, breaking
company rules, misconducting
left and right, all because
he is screaming to get canned
but is too scared to leave
on his own. But when
God gives you the boot, it's easy
to feel cheated, a little
bitter, a little dry. Lucifer
appreciates the patience
of his work counselor, Shirley.
"We'll find something," she
says. "Or maybe we can
school you in something."
Lucifer looks at her. "You
know," he says, "I've always
wanted to go into film. Directing.
I've always admired Chaplin.
Are you familiar with his work?"

II.

At night Lucifer burns
his dinner and eats it. He
writes long, narrative poems
of his hate for the world.
He alienates his lover with
seedless pomegranates and pity.
Lucifer explains to her, "Looking
for work does a number
on your self-esteem." Still,
she chooses to love him,
and he wonders how she
still can, pending his divorce,
pending his unemployment —
"Make use of your time," she says.
"It's a perfect opportunity
for you to write. Don't let
those bastards get to you.
Defeat them while you're
on their severance pay." He writes
more poems, love poems. The old
meters are no longer there, but
he keeps at it in a language
rough enough to please him.
He shows her one, and she
is happy. A small sign for her.
Even so, the despondency returns,
God's hard laugh and echo, "Get
your sorry ass out of here," and
worse, signing the resignation
to save face. Or else he hears
Sartre, or some other old,
dead existentialist friend

whisper, "You were never
a pianist if you ever quit
playing the piano." Lucifer
wonders whose joke is crueler —
God's or Sartre's — when all he
has is time, and everyone he knows
no longer has an appetite for
silent films, for a sentimentality
that opens a heart, a little
humor, a little gravity, a little
love.

Tom

When is the body a gift,
really? For this day's history
slips through my window:
the hazing citronella, the din
of mosquitoes, the sun-faded
raw sienna of sky bruising
to carbon, the registers of
classic rock radio and quarreling
children. It all slips through,
ashy and as heavy as wine
in the afternoon, and it could be
that it is only the town's
pre-rigor mortis settling down,
a body that enters and sleeps
upon the bones: Redding or
Rock Springs, could be Pocatello
for all I know, but whatever
the town, it is dying no quicker
than anything else that has
just smoldered, just cindered a little.

Save for that man across
my street, Tom Carlson, he
without his shirt, inching
the washing machine toward
the apartment's door-frame. From
this distance, I am with him,
shouldering the machine ajar,
and from this distance,
I know the room of his late
adolescence: the chin bar,
the dumb bells, and on
his dresser, green hair gel, photos
from Tahoe, no cologne. From
this distance, I am with him, inside

sharing beers, laughing, not talking
much, like some lesser brothers
who stayed put. No, I am just
a neighbor now closing a blind.

Wendy stands in the hollow of
shade of the open door. Her need
glazes even the light. She
knows that when Tom gets
this way, when he gets
this way, she'll soon slip
into her gown, crisp and textured,
and she'll curl upon the couch
and raise her arm to draw her husband
near, to draw his weight, warmed
with work, upon her. The ebbing,
the shivering twilight outside
cools the air as a cumulus grown heavy,
ungirdling with rain.

The Pink Palace

Here is an art
good enough to carry:
a Joseph Cornell
box. Take a photostat
of a Newport mansion,
wash it pink, cut
news-clips of a woman's
face, litter her face
as pieces of snow on
the mansion's grounds,
arrange some sticks
for trees, a background
mirror to flush
the depth and to catch
the looker looking.
And forget to name
the artwork, load
the elements in a blue
black box, a container
of surreal, stupid air,
confetti light, hardware,
and a woman's face
forming a drift. I wish
I had that pink
palace, that box
large enough
to house its want.

I Wish I Could Skate Across the Wide, Frozen River
— from lines by Joni Mitchell

As a schoolboy, I never understood
the geography of lakes, how only they
could have fingers. But I always
knew that rivers were full of hands,

hands of everyone dead and fantastical,
just beneath the flowing surface, and
even now, I will waver my hands above
the crest, nervous before I plunge them

into the cold, feeling nothing but force
and fluidity. Thus I remember
my bare hand on your brother's leg,
with everyone of us spread flat

on the frozen creek that clicked
solid from the sudden sub-zero night,
and all our hands on one another —
Tommy, Kenny, Elizabeth, Chuck, Mike,

Connie, you, me — or on the colding
ice. We each traded turns to watch
the denser, warmer water fall through
an open hollow of ice, listening

to the water's quickening, on its way
to confluences larger than us. We
stilled our bodies, sprawled and
seraphic, alive in the cold air,

connected by some great blood. I
would call it joy. Why else did we
endure that old exegesis of touch,
palm, and clasp? Our hands stayed

warm. But today I wish for a greater
river, frozen all the way through,
one mile wide, and I would skate
across it, gliding over all the hands

in the river, each one open and supple,
gliding over every last human
touch that broke surface and broke free.

The Drunken Comet

        Every comet I have seen
suffers itself like a poor drunk,
                even in the purest night

        in no-place, Idaho, its tail
skirting away to drift finer
                than the moonless film

        of star clutter, or even when
I was someplace, Tennant,
                California, with my lover, in

        perfect December-cold air,
even when the comet, meriting
                only some numb matrix

        of letters and numbers, failed
to pierce any magnitude
                beyond the puffs of our breathing.

        What good is any comet,
especially the sober ones
                that burn close to the sun

        tiding the earth with light,
except for the celestial fact
                everyone knows: a comet

        is a dirty snowball? And so
I cherish the drunken comet,
                the less universal disappointment

       that will come as I point
to some nebula still unspinning
              itself, and I say, *I think*

       that's it, Kimberly, knowing
I am wrong, way wrong, knowing
              that she is leaving me, knowing

       that the night and its weight
of every star of this winter
              solstice might kill me ere long,

       ere the return of a true comet
that would alight every
              nerve of the dead and blind them.

The Pope Arrives in Denver

The Pontiff, at 28,000 feet and falling,
one hour from Stapleton, recalls
his prayer for the children of Mexico City,
displeased with his poor phrasing
in Spanish — too much of the Catalan —
and above he watches the trace of comet
filament, striking the sky, an electric
confetti, becoming tears, these meteors,
and he looks upon the America beneath him,
the sundry violences upon the earth purpling
in the dark. On I-70, cars and buses are
strung, teenagers from Iowa or Detroit also
arriving in Denver, and on television
a white girl speaks of all this hope, how
it will stop the madness, the drugs,
the teen pregnancy. "I am from Cedar Rapids,"
she says. And the news producer decides
to quick edit all the teenagers she interviewed,
cueing up their hometowns like a line
across the continent: "I'm from Aurora,"
"I'm from Sedalia," "I'm from Cleveland,"
"I'm from Santa Barbara," "I'm from
Lincoln," "I'm from Abilene." The producer
headlines the segment, *Kids Across America*.
Instead, I am in Green River, Wyoming,
in a bad hotel, having just masturbated,
having just flushed my come down the toilet,
hating those moments afterward that confirm
only loneliness, and predictably I think
of my lover and these perils
of separation. After all, above me, above
these western overcast skies, the heavens
are sparkling, and southward, John Paul II
is kneeling and kissing the tarmac, and
surely love presently comes to someone

and his beloved, desecrating their bodies,
stilling them, as if there were no world, no
finer physics, no universe, save for what
seizes them, there, in that embrace, in that
nakedness, in that dark nowhere
everywhere about them. Where are
they from? I think they come from small places
on the atlas, small towns in Idaho, say
Eden, or say Kimberly, or someplace over there
on the map, over north, California. I
think they come from places near to me.

III. Beyond the Coast of Nashville, the Desert of Idaho

>Big Tiger had never had a map in his hand before, but he pretended to know all about maps and remarked airily, "I can't read all the names on this one because they are in English."
>
>Christian realized he would have to show his friend how to read a map. "The top is north," he said. "The little circles are towns and villages. Blue means rivers and lakes, and the thin lines are roads and the thick ones railways."
>
>"There's nothing at all here," said Big Tiger, pointing to one of the many white patches.
>
>"That means it's just desert," explained Christian. "You have to go into the desert to know what it looks like."
>
>— *Fritz Muhlenweg*

The Bad Cartographer

I have found the shape of my death:
emptying my pockets after a day
at the office — keys, pennies and dimes,
a lunch receipt, leafing out my billfold,

and a fist of cigars, cellophaned, and I
pull from them five paper rings
for my boy, and he wears them;
the smell of pressed tobacco on his fingers

remains through the evening. Of course,
it's a lie. He's two-thousand miles away,
stretches of longitudes that mark the familiar
disreputes: divorce and absence. Love's

topography, at least of what I've seen, is
of too many how-to-get-theres-from-here.
I take to my workshop and begin
a new map, abandoning the compassings

to some terra incognita, a simpler grid for my son,
a way for him to find the Chapultepec zoo
from his bedroom in Nashville, where
some benighted local animal, some American

cow, sleeps, and my son, warm with God,
will watch her rest. Is she dead, Daddy?
he will ask. This map I will embroider with bone
and distortion, drawing an inviolate pole where

everything must find relation, an imprint
of the pretense that history is of space
and time. Whose forgivenesses do I seek?
Whose maps will lead to me? But the stars —

yes, to chart their faring larcenies —
now the stars, yes, they're easy.

On the Maps of Creativity

On the maps of creativity, the behaviorist
locates liquid ideas and vortices that cusp
like the first tulips emerging through
the graveled winter dirt. Beyond
the grid, the only perfect circles he draws
are irresolution. A trigger, labeled
catastrophe, convulses, a fold that brings
a new starting point, a new plot of ground
for the seeding. Outside everything
lies inaccessible behavior, the name he
bequeaths infinity, where no root takes hold.

As I listen to my son mouth his new words,
I cannot chart exactly where the fold disappears.
Somewhere on the map, I stand, an X
asking, "How does a doggie go?" "Woof!
Woof!" His voice blooms above the subaqueous
meaning, curving forever from my mark.
I pray for only suppleness in his sounding. I pray,
even though I know that his trajectory
is a connection, that I should lift my son
and dance, his free hand open, grasping for me.

Traces

My child, in his room, is playing,
and I cannot tell whether he
is laughing or crying, but I will
not stir from my reading, for his joy,

as I imagine, over the leaves
of sycamore we found is his own,
and if his noise is the child's
grief, that, too, is his own. To be

truthful, I am afraid that I can
no longer restore comfort out of pain.
Still, I know I will seek in the broad
ways whom my soul loves, and I

retrieve one trick I learned young,
so that I do rise and go. I mix
sugar milk and take paper and matches
into his room. *Here,* I tell him,

I have something to show you. With
the liquid, he traces circles
with his finger upon the paper, and I
lay my hand over his hand, to feel

the movement of what he has in mind.
The circles, I think, become smoother,
rounder, smaller. I say, *Okay,
let's let the paper dry,* and

I return to my reading, and he
to his quieter play. And it is fear
again: how a father dreams of
the drowning child he can never save,

the child's face disappearing
in a swallow of silt, how a father
plays with combustible materials
and their traces — fire and ash — that

will leave nothing but the child's
tiny bones. It is fear because I know
my son will come to me, asking
if it is ready, and I will have

to say yes. I will light the match
beneath the paper, and from nothing
will appear maybe something like a face,
something like my own face,

fevered, blistered, blackening faster
than the paper, or the design becomes
my child's face in a cry or a laugh,
calling out someone else's name.

The Good Uncle

Is there any better word:
avuncular? A word as easy
as I can lift my niece,
or nephew, with a recklessness
their fathers reserve. Me,
on Thanksgivings, I bring home
the pretty woman from Florida, and outside
I build the children a snow fort
and throw snow balls at them,
hard. After dinner, I phone
my son, their age, and each
hears my boy recite
the same joke two thousand miles
away. My son tells them
he's eaten oysters and whale meat
for dinner, and I tell his cousins
it's true. Of course, when I carry
five-year-old Nadine, the youngest,
to bed, when she gives me
dog-lick kisses, it is my boy
I am lifting, carrying him through
such hard and distant corridors,
until I would shore him upon
his bed. When I leave Nadine's room
the new woman I love comments
to my parents how these children
love me. I tell her it is nothing.
But when I hold Nadine, she is
everything, and every color, every
sound, is as primary and as lasting
as the fist of her tiny hand
uncurling itself from my neck,
unhitched from her Uncle Jimmy.

In the Hospital of Broken Rules: Optic Ward, Children's Wing

While the doctor follows her rounds,
she thinks how disease is changeless:

the seven-year-old boy who clings
into himself, crying "Unfair," his eyes

struck crossed, forever; the preschooler
who insists on a blue marble to replace the brown

eye the scissors poked out, to match
the eyes of her border collie, Rex;

or the ten-year-old boy who didn't know
better than to accept his brother's dare,

as he looked into the solar eclipse.
The doctor, who has walked through life

up till this moment never breaking
a rule, touches the boy's cheek,

brushes the hair that never lies flat,
saying once more, "You shouldn't

have done that," and the doctor leaves
for the paralysis case in the bicycle ward.

The boy looks down, his bad eye a wild,
white sun, the corona he saw still printed

in the vision of his good eye. Today,
in his reading exercise, he has learned

that corona really means "crown" and that
everything round, every eye, contains its own

corona, a white sliver eclipsed inside the iris.

Girl at the Hotel Exile

These Sundays I watch Father practice on the tennis court; it is
an indulgence of his I humor. I like it anyway: the red, Hawai'ian

clay, the yellow balls, the white shorts, and the brown skin are
movie colors. I drink Cokes. Life, I tell my father, is full of hotels.

Only Mother takes the defeat hard, stays indoors, still cursing
the effete generals and the communist students. Now that I

want to be an American, now that I wear make-up even though
I am but thirteen, I buy sexy novels. I read

my family's story in *The National Enquirer*. What I could tell
would sell big: how Mother dances through the kitchen naked

and drunk; how Father has taken to situation-comedies;
how they embraced me after we arrived, after I had broken

open my doll's head, revealing the tiny diamonds I had smuggled
from the palace, Mother crying, *My Jewel, my Jewel*.

The story I know is something else. That my parents no longer love
is nothing. Me, I am only watching them in this warm, American

paradise. We are wealthy. I am not so young. I know a boy
at the swimming pool: his skin is browner than mine.

Gloucester and Edgar at Dover

A boy like you must carry gratitude
this far: lead father to the mad
sea's hem and bleed his pity.

Vacations and their atlases
are what you remember.
"Smile, Son," he used to say,
snapping the Instamatic to fill
album titles: "Edgar at Yellowood,
Idaho, 1973," or "Edgar's First Canoe
Ride, near Nashville, October 1971."
Father hit and hit you for not wearing
the life preserver. You were six.
It did not matter. You understood
love then: the leaves turned,
the last south wind of summer slapped
water, father's laughter rimmed
the air with apple tobacco.

You can remember that now, even
in this lousy weather, even as you
tell the old man, the old fool, to jump.

The Second Sky

To my son, whom I left, I would leave
a second sky, cleansed of emollience and blue,
and still large, glacial, familial.
I am lying. That is the sky I want,
without the bearing of my escape,
without any direction save outwardness,
without absences. And for the real sky,
above us, I will outline its orientations
and demarcations for my son, all
the calibrations of familiarity so that
he knows the Latin names of the little
bear or the seven sisters, so that
he can predict the mooring of Venus
against the horizon. Everything I write
him will be of expanses and homecomings
and fair readings, somethings of promise,
and — say it — somethings of love.

IV. Florida, Where We Are Heading

> Love that gives us ourselves, in the world known to all
> new techniques for the healing of a wound,
> and the unknown world. One life, or the faring stars.
>
> — *Muriel Rukeyser*

Lover's Key, Florida

> And a man in love, besides, is always fearful.
> So I decided to give myself a reason
> To have a grievance.
> — Ovid

Easy arrivals, Ovid, old friend,
my grievance is with them. The tide
will soon out, and the water will
recede and leave the destitute clutter
my lover and I will rummage
and recast. How old are these shells,
these dolphin bones, still white?
Recent, I must think. At this beach,
the gulf's modest economies
relinquish their capital: sea grass,
urchins, sibilant matter. The gulf,
you would think, has in it a voice
— a pain — that covers everything.

Only the sound itself is everything:
a Caspian Tern chitting, or de Leon's
Spanish marking, or today, an
American sighing, "This is nice.
This is some beach." Sounding
insists on repetition. How else are we
to be fixed, if not by echolocation?

My beloved covers her skin with sun
block, draws out a towel, sits,
and enjoys herself — it's an ocean,
not a waterfall, after all. She turns
to me. "Need some? It's Florida,
you know," and she points
to the sun, which touches and burns
everything white, so that it becomes

necessary for me to remember
snow, an Idaho snow that once
could cover everything, quiet
everything in my childhood.

"Sure," I tell her, "I'll take some."
While I am grateful, I sometimes wish
to lie in snow, which also bleaches
and preserves the body, if it is
a dry snow, if it stays cold
enough long enough.

The Cartography of Oranges
— for Beverly

In everyone's junior-high-school geography class,
>   the teacher takes an orange, and says,
>>   "Imagine this orange as the world,
or rather, as a model of the world. We call that model

a globe." The geography teacher cuts the orange in half,
>   and he dips the halves in water to kill
>>   the scent, to preserve our more virginal
senses. After he scoops out the fruit, he carefully shows

us the hollows of each half. "This," he says, "is what
>   happened to the globe when Mercator
>>   got his hands on it." As the teacher
smashes the orange on the wax-papered desk, we students

try hard not to think of the hand of God at that moment,
>   while the hand of this teacher lifts
>>   the flattened peel for us to witness.
"See? See what the world becomes now?" We sit. We are

watching our teacher, like any such teacher, he having risen
>   to a position beyond his talents. We
>>   are witnessing, bearing his anger.
"See? What lesson does this experiment tell you about maps?"

I confess that everything I have learned about the science
>   of cartography began with oranges,
>>   and everything I have learned
about sex, and therefore love, began with oranges. For with

oranges, I learned how any map is a lie of location, a slip
>   of language that seduces me to come
>>   near the surface of where I might
become certain of where I am exactly. For with oranges, I

65

understand the globe of passion. Beneath my touching its skin,
naturally, there is flesh, secretive and
arterial, and water, and I can taste it,
even before I open the orange, even before the map tells me

how to get there.

The Residual Boy

Your love makes no difference —
I have spent life climbing trees,
lacquered in ambient Idaho
light, petting all the bad

Dobermans in the neighborhood,
spitting for spit's sake,
diving head first, and looking
at all the pretty girls, new
and limbed in their bikinis,

their breasts open and watery
dream, their ease so enviable
that I splash them, to hear
their shouts, their name-calling,

to see their bodies move,
to receive their looks, their
flushed and tanned faces.
Later I will fall somewhere
in the world, with no good place

to spit. I will fall as easy
as slipping into the coldest lake,
naked, midnight, immersing
fully, then surfacing, calling

for you to join me. I will
fall and slip into water,
letting it cover me with every
male glimmering light,
and the moon upon the surface

above me forever multiplying
and dividing. I will disappear,
holding my breath, waiting
for you to turn chicken

and call out my name, even
when you know better. I will
surface, laughing low, a little
cruel, and in the black, you
can see my smile, my teeth,

and I will raise my head and
cast forth from my mouth
a spout of water. I will disappear
with a kick, moving slow,

staying everything but my pounding
heart, as I find some
easy grounding, a siltless
landing, smoothed with night
pearls, fresh-water shells,

quick water, and above, this world
for you is calming, black,
the only stirring some wind,
a mist lowing upon the lake.

My Grand Cayman Dog

It wouldn't have been accidental, landing
at this intersection, this quickened and impossible
heat. What power brought us? What forsaken
Caribbean god managed me here, alive,
with you and this dog, an escapee, a contingent
native, diseased and ill-fed? In my hand

a little meat, a lure. I wave my hand
near her muzzle. "Here girl," I say, to land
her close to me. I could just grab her, a contingent
plan, and toss her in the car, make possible
a new refuge for her, take her to live
in the George Town humane shelter, for her sake.

Rather, I wish to show patience, to forsake
my American habitudes. She rises, licks my hand,
and I pet her, smile to you. We are alive,
edgy and giddy in this blue vacationland,
all alive, and I can't say how it's possible:
this black stray, me, you, all contingencies

on this bank-full and bankrupt isle, contingent
Grand Cayman, Great Britain's moneyed keepsake.
Yet, my gesture matters, I believe — a possibility,
a retrieval — cupping hamburger in my hand,
too much for the dog to eat. How hard the land
between us, how narrow. I whisper, "Dog, live

a little, remove yourself from traffic, come and live
with us a little." An American contingency
we have become: one resident, one island
native, and me, a visitor. For this dog's sake
our simple wish is to play it a new hand,
or, a quieter death in the shelter. It's possible

now, because she eats a little more, impossible
now, because she's a little trusting. Enlivened,
she barks, a second stray arrives, sniffs my hand,
and takes the rest. They bolt. We've no contingent
plans. A Caymanian watches us forsaken
Americans. "Dear Jesus," he thinks, "such fools land

here. Give dogs hand-outs and expect them to live
for you? Impossible! Mongrels steal for their own sake.
Godless, such contingent love on our God-blessed land."

In fifth position,

the lift and bend of your arms,
the cradle of your spine, the line
of your neck wisped with hair,
and your *sur le cou-de-pied* is so slow
and deep that I think gravity
is glory, as you open your hip
to rise, a leg into *passè*.
At the *barre*, I watch
you in the mirrors, and I catch
my own posture, that even my chest
has lifted, settled in its own
stillness. Every shadow tells me
I am ready to move. This time,
you simply do not wish to teach
me, to correct anything,
to explain the space I occupy.
For in the most patient of loves,
you might direct me through the music
and its valence of desires,
but you cannot suffer such slowness,
not in this time, not in this movement.

A Little Gershwin

Purple everything
on stage, except for the blue
spotlight on the bare
chair,
and the woman
and the man who dance.
They are waves.
They are lovers.
They are waves.
And every light is purple,
silvering blue on them,
except her arms
that are brown
and her hands
that are brown
and that cup the air
with such weight.

At the dance's end
I ask you, "Was
that really you?"
"Yes," you say,
and your hands
and their fluencies
bring me to you,
and your hands
fan and glide
over my back.
I am growing
wings.

Her Disrobing

      She has said, "In dance, there is always gravity,
           for movement is a continual exchange of weight.
If you're doing it right, it is as if nothing touches ground.
      To rise, you must lower yourself toward earth.
You must think down. You must humble your body."

      I do not recall her movements as desperate, but
           I think of her raw doomed pull inside the music,
down to a place where pulse and breath have stopped.
      She liked it that way, dance as a sculpting of space,
of stealing shape out of nothing: her arm curved

      overhead in the dark, her eyes and chin tilted
           down, even her hair across her face still. Tonight,
her dance might have become something for the men
      along her life, or for me, this new man who might be
another punishment for the men she knew before.

      Before me, her disrobing is a simple, quiet slip,
           upon which a crinkle of cotton is the only
falling, the only capture in the air, and her nakedness
      stuns me. I cannot breathe against this turn and drop
of her knee, as she sweeps her body beneath the covers,

      powerful, a sexual angel. In her, I swear the music
           must be of something ugly, the body accustomed
to a pain, and sometimes, too, when she hovers
      above my body, so still that I am alone, the sound must
be of laughter, of one wing extending and lowing.

~ Burial

> At the center of that pleasure was the determination that other people must relinquish her body as she herself would.
> — *Gerri Reaves*

Because the Upshur County Coroner's Code
4(d) holds that no death within the county's
dominion can be certified without the coroner's
or a state-licensed examiner's or a physician's
signature, I will have to keep your promise
that your bastard death remain illegitimate,
to transport your body a thousand miles south
to the mangrove fraying with Spanish moss,
to the humus heating even at night
with decay, to the mounding dirt, to the air
rotting with water and mold, to the carnivorous
ants. The corpse that I will lay upon this ground
will have abandoned its weight, and I will
whisper to its insentient ear words about
birds feeding from the unburrowing worms,
about this good, felonious life, about what I
cannot relinquish of the body. Or rather,
I will cup from the earth a fist of grass
and sprinkle the grass upon its hair, and years
later, when some state's authorities will
recover the remains, some teeth, a pelvis bone,
they will find a shock of peat grass
the color of your living hair. I am not
foretelling the truth. That body will be
carpeted with the clutter of forested debris,
but nothing will happen, except for the old,
additioned loss, the incremental silence,
unauthorized, as indomitable as the great
need of the body to die, simply to die.

Hurricane. North Dakota

The morning the storm breaches
shore, on the television news, wind
surfers hinge their bodies to sails,
pink and yellow running along
a brackening of sky and horizon,
and one says to the newscaster,
We're not crazy, squinting against
the sheets of rain and camera
light. *You know, it's the only way
man can fly.*
                    And later,
after the reprieve of violent low
pressure, above the spit of chain saws
and limb shredders, rise stories
of returning to a world no one
left: the one heirloom preserved,
the good national guardsmen
who ward away the looters, the litany
of frozen meats gone bad, the newly
uncaged conures and amazon parrots
of Florida that scatter upon the areca
palms. All the colors return aquatic.
Thus, in the hurricane season,
I think of you, my love.

Or more true, I remember
North Dakota, where wind suffers
itself no long, desirous stillness.
Somewhere there, in a field
risen with prairie grass, light
two macaws upon a cottonwood tree.
This tree is denuded but for the midnight
curve of these birds. I have
to think of such things, because
you have left this Idaho

or that North Dakota, because simply
you are far from me. I have
to think of such things, as unreal
as the starry faces of those escapees,
to think of their feathers, blue,
freighted with African air, of how
crushing it is for the exotic
to have any resiliency.

She Sleeps Under Florida

At the Metro-Dade Cultural Center
Plaza, she and I stand before
the directory for the Museum of Fine
Arts, deciphering the signage
that would deliver us to that X that says,
You Are Here. And we are.
What I want is the quickest track
out, the right directions to escape
the paintings of the "Self-Identified Catholic,
Homosexual, Full-Blown AIDS-Afflicted,
Mexican" artist, who has known personally
— this, too, from the museum brochure —
Madonna and Andy Warhol while
he lived in New York City, who seems
to know his face only, primitive and
feminine in colors so hard and loveless
that I am dizzy with roses, blood,
crucifixes, and belabored pity. What
I want is to leave, to feel the foreign
air outside that will place me
at some here, some X, any west
of now, that will transport me
to any California on the move. Yet,
she is even more bored than I,
for she has lived Florida so long
that whatever is Latin, maenadic,
or tortured, is nothing new. Having
lived Florida, she has not found
much at rest with the west I have
occupied, the west that is burning
and flaking off from the continental
drift of unhappy Americans, who have
nothing left except for some material
to burn, some hard land to raze.
Rather, she chooses to sleep under

a Florida, or rather, a greater Miami
she loves, and the map she draws
in her sleep lacks names, scales,
and legends, but is crayoned coral,
lime, blue, tangerine, crayoned with
colors no lover could really apprehend.

What Is Uncharted Remains

        America has never been that much
of a comfort for me, even
        in my childhood maps, the states
            veined and colored body parts
as puzzle pieces, and every edge

        holding its integrity, pushing
to the Pacific. Even those maps
        weren't much help in finding
missing places. This America where

        I love you is a country on the air,
an electronic grid careening no-
        where, until some of us sift through,
landing in Ocala, Seattle, or this

        West Virginia, where you are showering
in lotions and steamy water, after
        I have spilled my semen in you.
            I am lying on your bed, hearing
the water run, and you are standing or

        kneeling, massaging your legs, a soft
pliè, open to the cascading.
        The water sweats upon your face.
Love, your body is the shape

        of persuasion, and I know its
impossible geographies: near the rose
        of your areola, and there my mouth
        is there, over the shadowed freckles
that my lips have wished to claim.

    About us, the Americas sound
their diminishments, photonic and noisy
        and permanent. There is no place
for answering. Here, in this house,

    you are in the next room, and I am
imagining you, imagining against
        the grid, gathering words for hard times,
trying to possess one human telling

    of how I love the fierce rise
of your body, its blue moment that does
        not dissipate. Sitting, you bend
    with your own hands on your calf,
kneading, and the smell of our sex

    flows from you, traces of oil, spin,
and come, a film expanding
        in its dissolution, an undiscovered
continent adrift and disappearing.

    American and alone, I have to wonder
if I am the last one in the house.
        No, I hear you singing I don't know
what. And in the other room,

    the lovebirds are calling, roused
in the dark, calling to calm away
        the fearing, each one flashing its own
    color, a trembling picture coming
alive and perishing, as these uncharted

    sounds find me. I will sing back
in any old note, any man's song
        of shoring and love, a sound for you,
an answer, a calling, a founding.

Florida, at the End of Time

I have to remind myself
        humanity is a recent thing
                that dares not understand
its impossible erasure, dares

not land on this Florida,
        its beach and universe where
                everything has an end. Nor
do I. Love, do you regard

the water and its quiet
        pliabilities? I do. Or do
                you think of a land unmoored
in grass, or of an oceanic

desert with Hollywood sand,
        or of a mountain crested
                upon tectonic plates? Earth?
Water? Air? Fire? Florida?

Such places our bodies become
        sub-mineral. There, our bodies
                beckon to some elemental
signature, an encrypted

memory of origin where
        every wind has its vapory
                consciousness, where every
wind moves us to sex, love,

animation, retirement. In
        such places, such in-between
                lands and waters and their
arrested evolutions, such

places with and without Eden,
        with and without beginning,
                the keener one between us
stops during our walk along

this South Florida beach,
        stops upon a place stilled
                on the common maps,
and kneels to trace clouds

and cormorants in the sand.
        In such places — above us
                in the twilight, gulls
call to their mates, and

due north of us, the lights
        of Miami Beach multiply,
                a soft cartoon foregrounded
on dredged sand — and in such

places, the wind tarries
        across our skin. After
                I am lost remembering what
shutter speed will suffuse

this kind of light, deciphering
        the camera's trick of capture,
                I look upon you, my beloved,
and release the snapshot:

lust itself is rescue against time.
        Your skin, unto which I
                surrender, tells me I am not
a being but a place, tells me

        how mostly happy is any one
                so near this edge of waiting.

The Bougainvillea, Your Black Dress

> After all, the sky flashes, the great sea yearns,
> we ourselves flash and yearn ...
> — *John Berryman*

After the detonate wind, after the hurricane
    three years ago, you saved the bougainvillea,
        sheering the broken limbs, untangling
the knotted veins for more light. You told me

how the leaves, ankle-deep, were papery,
    clean, like the discarded wings of insects.
        For two days, your hands were swollen,
for the thick, tumorous net of thorns pierced

through the layers of your gloves. Surely,
    I think, your lover then held your hands,
        coveting those wounds he could
tend, and he nearly wept as he salved

your palms. The beauty is in the bougainvillea's
    deformity, its danger, you said. Today, I
        asked for this, all of this, over the phone,
while on your line harps played on the radio,

either Debussy or Ravel or Faurè, we could
    not name. The music sounded like a Degas
        woman shadowed by candle, or you
in your black dress, before the bougainvillea,

a sea of outrageous coral, too full and
    swollen, a renovation of sex and
        abundance, a swirling of a hunger
you could live by. When you say touch does not

make beauty repulsive, you are right.
        Love, all my life, my body has been
                impatient, ambient only with want.
When you wear your black dress — the seam

that splits at your breasts, the extravagance
        of your skin and hair — I see a woman
                dressed in the last sensible idea,
a happiness distinct from melancholy. Yes,

beauty is not an island, but a siren,
        scorching the sky with flash and
                yearn, and we ourselves are flashing
and yearning. And if we lose a little blood

on a twist of thorns? And if we become
        a little infected? When you wear your
                black dress, I will come to you,
ungloved.

Island Park: Midnight

       Island Park is the wrong name
for this place. At Island Park,
           you should be below the subtropics,

     having just retired the riggings
because the wind frayed slack
           and the boat is drifting. At Island

     Park, you should be falling upon
each island by accident, or each one
           coming to you, whole, with

     ungardened aviaries. You should
be combing the evening sky, netting
           all the low, close planets buoyant

     on the Atlantic, so calm
even the air becomes a warm verb:
           wither, weather, wuther.

     But Island Park is in Idaho,
and beneath a December
           new moon, Island Park is just

     a snow field, between river and
reservoir, a convulse of lava that rose
           and shivered solid. Still, with

     our friends, you and I cannot believe
our luck, leaning heavy on our ski
           poles, resting. Over the black

     crests and falls of snow, beneath
the black crystalline clouds, only
           the stars are clear, only our

       shadowed bodies a sure thing.
I can tell you are looking at me.
               I am not surprised to be shorn

       there, to be reckoned as a moment
to such stillness, to be made
               by your memory, as if all along

       I had lain there in this cold Idaho,
newly risen from this male-steeped
               darkness, unclaimed for so long,

       until now.

About the author

James Brock, an Idaho native, landed in Florida after serving as an academic Kelly Girl for ten years, having taught at universities in Indiana, Tennessee, Idaho, Pennsylvania, and Miami. *nearly Florida* is his second book of poetry. His first book was *The Sunshine Mine Disaster*, published by University of Idaho Press. For his poetry, he has won fellowships from the National Endowment of the Arts, the Alex Haley Foundation, the Tennessee Arts Commission, and the Idaho Commission for the Arts. He now leads the Writing Program at Florida Gulf Coast University in Fort Myers, where he enjoys dance, birding, and film.

FLORIDA POETRY SERIES

ANHINGA PRESS

The Secret History of Water
Silvia Curbelo, 1997

Braid
Mia Leonin, 1999

nearly Florida
James Brock, 2000